First published July 2004

Ridgehill Publishing,
32 Ridgehill,
Henleaze,
Bristol
BS9 4SB

Tel: +44 (0) 117 962 2670
Fax: +44 (0) 117 962 28344
www.ridgehillpublishing.com

ISBN: 1-84556-098-1

Selected Sound Discovery® Snappy Lesson Plans

at Steps 1, 2 and 3A

Trudy Wainwright
Advanced Skills Teacher

Contents

This selection of lesson plans is written to be used in conjunction with Sound Discovery Words and Sentences Part1.

To find out where to start teaching on the programme, the teacher or Teaching Assistant needs to assess the children (whole class or group) using the appropriate Sound Discovery Placement test (for Step 1 and 2, for Step 3A or Step 3B). This can be administered to a group as a spelling test or as an individual reading test.

When the first error is made, read off the Sound Discovery Step at the end of the line. The teaching starts at this Sound Discovery Step e.g. when a child writes 'tet' for 'tent' – start teaching at Step 1.3

These sessions of 'Snappy Lesson' are planned to last for 20-30 minutes with both reading and spelling being taught in one lesson.

A blank 'Snappy Lesson' planning grid and the phonic progression for the lesson plans are also included. Should you wish to write your own plan to supplement those in this selection, you can use this blank grid and Sound Discovery Words and Sentences Part1

Sound Discovery® Snappy Lesson Plans for
Words And Sentences Handbook Part 1

The 'Snappy Lesson' plans included in this pack are listed below. There are
29 lesson plans included. If you require others, it is possible to generate
your own plans by using the blank template and 'Words and Sentences
Part 1'.

Step	Phonemes	Pages
Step 1	Alphabet Phonemes	
1.1	3 phonemes c-v-c	1
1.3	4 phonemes end consonant clusters	2
1.4	4 phonemes initial consonant clusters	3
1.5	5 phonemes initial and end consonant clusters	4
Step 2	Consonant & Vowel Digraphs	
2.1	Consonant digraphs th, sh, ch, ng	5, 6, 7, 8
2.2	Vowel digraphs ai, ee, ie, oa, ue	9, 10, 11, 12, 13
2.3	Vowel controlled r: ar, er, or	14, 15, 16
Step 3A	Main Alternative Vowel Spellings	
3A.2	/ai/ as ai, ay, a-e (ey)	17, 18, 19
3A.4	/ie/ as ie, y, igh, i-e, i	20, 21, 22, 23, 24
3A.5	/oa/ as oa, ow, o-e, o	25, 26, 27, 28
3A.9	/or/ as or (au, aw, al)	29

Snappy Lesson Plan
Phoneme

Sound Discovery Step

Learning Objective:
Success Critieria:

Reading | Spelling

Reading	Spelling
1. **Review Sounds** (show as a pack)	7. **Sound Dictation**
2.**Focus Sounds:**	8. **Focus Sounds:**
3. **Blending (oral) Robot Speech:**	9. **Phoneme Fingers:**
4. **Manipulating Sounds:**	
5. **Reading Words**	10. **Word Dictation** (tap and write)
6. **Reading Sentences** (and controlled texts)	11. **Sentence Dictation** (Pupils read words and sentences at the end)

Comments (to inform next plan and IEP)

3 Phoneme words using alphabet phonemes

Learning Objective: to blend and segment three phoneme words using alphabet phonemes
Success Criteria: to read three phoneme words and write dictated words and a sentence with 100% accuracy.

Reading	Spelling
1. Review Sounds (show as a pack) • s, a, t, i, p, n, c, e, h, r, m, d	**7. Sound Dictation** • h, r, m, n
2. Focus Sounds: r, m, n • With the phonemes play the 'grab game'. With the cards on the table the teacher says a sound and the pupils grab for the letter.	**8. Focus Sounds**: r, m, n • The teacher checks the letter formation for the correct start point, exit stroke and place on the line.
3. Blending (oral) **Robot Speech**: • Teacher says sounds 'r-a-t', pupils say word 'rat'. Repeat for pin, tap, man, hat, can	**9. Phoneme Fingers**: The teacher says a word and the pupils flick fingers for each sound in p-i-n, t-a-p, m-a-n, h-a-t, c-a-n

4. Manipulating Sounds: With vowels a, e, i, o, u at the top of the board and consonants at the bottom, the teacher says a word. The pupils fold 'phoneme fingers' and flick a finger up for each phoneme in the word. One child comes up and makes the word. The teacher says the next word. The next child, after flicking 'phoneme fingers' for the new word, changes 1 sound (or 2), makes the word and reads the new word.
• Today work on pit, pin, tin, tan, ten, hen or rat, ran, man, mat, met, set

Reading	Spelling
5. Reading Words (read as a pack) See Sound Discovery Step 1.1 E.g. sat, pat, pin, pit, tip, tap, tan, sit	**10. Word Dictation** (tap and write) See Sound Discovery Step 1.1 E.g. sat, pat, pin, pit, tip, tap, tan,
6. Reading Sentences (and controlled texts) I tap the tin. It is a pin. I tip the pan. I sit on it.	**11. Sentence Dictation** (pupils read words and sentences at the end) I tap the tin. It is a pin. I tip the pan. I sit on it.

Comments (to inform next plan and IEP)

Snappy Lesson Plan   Sound Discovery Step 1.3

4 Phoneme words with end consonant clusters

Learning Objective: to blend and segment 4 phoneme words with end consonant clusters

Success Criteria: to read 4 phoneme words and to write from dictation 4 phoneme words and sentences with 100% accuracy.

Reading	Spelling
1. Review Sounds (show as a pack) c, e, h, r, m, g, o, u, l, f, b	**7. Sound Dictation** c, d, g
2. Focus Sounds: g, d: With the phonemes play the 'grab game'. With the cards on the table the teacher says a sound and the pupils grab for the letter.	**8. Focus Sounds:** g, d: The teacher checks the letter formation for the correct start point, exit stroke and place on the line.
3. Blending (oral) Robot Speech: The teacher says the sounds l-a-m-p, the pupils listen and say the word for lamp, tent, mist, lost lump, hand	**9. Phoneme Fingers:** The teacher says a word, the pupils flick fingers for each sound in l-a-m-p, t-e-n-t, m-i-s-t, l-o-s-t l-u-m-p, h-a-n-d
4. Manipulating Sounds: With vowels a, e, i, o, u at the top of the board and consonants at the bottom, the teacher says a word. The pupils fold 'phoneme fingers' and flick a finger up for each phoneme in the word. One child comes up and makes the word. The teacher says the next word. The next child, after flicking 'phoneme fingers' for the new word, changes 1 sound (or 2), makes the word and reads the new word. • Today work on: ten, tent, sent, bent, bend, band	
5. Reading Words (read from a pack) • See Sound Discovery Step 1.3: mend, lamp, lost, sent, sand, hand	**10. Word Dictation** (tap and write) See Sound Discovery Step 1.3: mend, lamp, lost, sent, sand, hand
6. Reading Sentences (and controlled texts) • He has lost his pen. • I can mend this lamp. • Sam went up on the box, • The tent bent in the wind. • The man is in the band.	**11. Sentence Dictation** (pupils read words and sentences at the end) • He has lost his pen. • I can mend this lamp. • Sam went up on the box, • The tent bent in the wind. • The man is in the band.

Comments (to inform next plan and IEP)

Snappy Lesson Plan   Sound Discovery Step 1.4

4 Phoneme words with initial consonant clusters

Learning Objective: to blend and segment 4 phoneme words with initial consonant clusters.

Success Critieria: to read 4 phoneme words and to write from dictation 4 phoneme words and sentences with 100 % accuracy.

Reading	Spelling
1. Review Sounds (show as a pack) c, h, r, m, d, g, o, u, l, b	**7. Sound Dictation** r, m, d
2. Focus Sounds: r, m, d: With the phonemes play the 'grab game'. With the cards on the table the teacher says a sound and the pupils grab for the letter.	**8. Focus Sounds**: r, m, d • The teacher checks the letter formation for the correct start point, exit stroke and place on the line.
3. Blending (oral) Robot Speech: The teacher says the sounds 'p-r-a-m', the pupils listen and say the word for pram, spot, plan, frog, grab, spin	**9. Phoneme Fingers**: The teacher says a word, the pupils flick fingers for each sound in p-r-a-m, s-p-o-t, p-l-a-n, f-r-o-g, g-r-a-b, s-p-i-n
4. Manipulating Sounds: With vowels a, e, i, o, u at the top of the board and consonants at the bottom, the teacher says a word. The pupils fold 'phoneme fingers' and flick a finger up for each phoneme in the word. One child comes up and makes the word. The teacher says the next word. The next child, after flicking 'phoneme fingers' for the new word, changes 1 sound (or 2), makes the word and reads the new word. • Today work on pin, pit, spit, spat, spot or rat, ran, trap, trip, trot, tram	
5. Reading Words (read from a pack) See Sound Discovery Step 1.4 E.g. plan, trip, spot, plum, step, pram	**11. Word Dictation** (tap and write) See Sound Discovery Step 1.4 E.g. plan, trip, spot, plum, step, pram
6. Reading Sentences (and controlled texts) See Sound Discovery Step 1.4 The rat ran into the trap. The bag is flat. I can snap this bent twig. He must not slip on the wet ramp. I went up the step.	**12. Sentence Dictation** (Pupils read words and sentences at the end) See Sound Discovery Step 1.4 The rat ran into the trap. The bag is flat. I can snap the bent twig. He must not slip on the wet ramp. I went up the step.
Comments (to inform next plan and IEP)	

5 Phoneme words with initial and end consonant clusters

Learning Objective: to blend and segment 5 phoneme words with initial and end consonant clusters.
Success Critieria: to read 5 phoneme words and to write from dictation 5 phoneme words and sentences with 100 % accuracy.

Reading	Spelling
1. Review Sounds (show as a pack) e, r, m, d, g, o, u, l, b, y,	**7. Sound Dictation** e, m, y
2. Focus Sounds: e, n, y • With the phonemes play the 'grab game'. With the cards on the table the teacher says a sound and the pupils grab for the letter.	**8. Focus Sounds**: e, n, y • The teacher checks the letter formation for the correct start point, exit stroke and place on the line.
3. Blending (oral) Robot Speech: The teacher says the sounds 's-t-a-m-p', the pupils listen and say the word for stamp, spend, plant, frost, grasp, spins	**9. Phoneme Fingers**: The teacher says a word, the pupils flick fingers for each sound in p-r-o-p-s, s-p-o-t-s, p-l-a-n-t, f-r-o-s-t, g-r-a-s-p

4. Manipulating Sounds: With vowels a, e, i, o, u at the top of the board and consonants at the bottom, the teacher says a word. The pupils fold 'phoneme fingers' and flick a finger up for each phoneme in the word. One child comes up and makes the word. The teacher says the next word. The next child, after flicking 'phoneme fingers' for the new word, changes 1 sound (or 2), makes the word and reads the new word.
• Today work on bend, bends, bands, sands, stands, stamp

Reading	Spelling
5. Reading Words (read from a pack) See Sound Discovery Step 1.5 E.g. stamp, spend, plant, frost, grasp,	**11. Word Dictation** (tap and write) See Sound Discovery Step 1.5 E.g. stamp, spend, plant, frost, grasp,
6. Reading Sentences (and controlled texts) See Sound Discovery Step 1.4 I plant a bulb in a pot. Tom can grasp the can. The frost is on the step. I stamp on the ant.	**12. Sentence Dictation** (Pupils read words and sentences at the end) See Sound Discovery Step 1.4 I plant a bulb in a pot. Tom can grasp the can. The frost is on the step. I stamp on the ant.

Comments (to inform next plan and IEP)

Ridgehill Publishing© Tel (+44 or 0) 117 9622670
www.ridgehillpublishing.com

Snappy Lesson Pl... **Sound Discovery Step 2.1**
Consonant Digrap...

Learning Objective: to b... the consonant digraph /th/.
Success Critieria: to rea... ...nant digraph /th/ and write from dictation /th/ words and sentence... ... ... acy.

Reading	Spelling
1. Review Sounds (show as a pack) sh, ch, th, ng	**7. Sound Dictation** sh, ch, th, ng
2. Focus Sound: th • With the consonant digraphs play the 'grab game'. With the cards on the table the teacher says a sound and the pupils grab for the grapheme.	**8. Focus Sound: th** • The teacher checks the letter formation for the correct start point, exit stroke and place on the line.
3. Blending (oral) **Robot Speech:** The teacher says sounds m-o-th, the pupils listen and say the word for moth, broth, with	**9. Phoneme Fingers:** Teacher says a word, pupils flick fingers for each sound in m-o-th, b-r-o-th, w-i-th
4. Manipulating Sounds: With vowels a, e, i, o, u at the top of the board and consonants at the bottom, the teacher says a word. The pupils fold 'phoneme fingers' and flick a finger up for each phoneme in the word. One child comes up and makes the word. The teacher says the next word. The next child, after flicking 'phoneme fingers' for the new word, changes 1 sound (or 2), makes the word and reads the new word. • Today work on with, this, thin, then, than	
5. Reading Words (read from a pack) See Sound Discovery Step 2.1 e.g. moth, with, smith, thing, thump	**10. Word Dictation** (tap and write) See Sound Discovery Step 2.1 E.g. moth, with, smith, thing, thump
6. Reading Sentences (and controlled texts) That pen is red. This moth is black. The thin man sat on the step. I must not thump the desk.	**11. Sentence Dictation** (pupils read words and sentences at the end) That pen is red. This moth is black. The thin man sat on the step. I must not thump the desk.
Comments (to inform next plan and IEP)	

Consonant Digraph sh

Learning Objective: to blend and segment 3 & 4 phoneme words with consonant digraph /sh/
Success Critieria: to read 3 and 4 phoneme words and sentences with the consonant digraph /sh/ and to write dictated /sh/ words and sentences with 100 % accuracy.

Reading	Spelling
1. Review Sounds sh, ch, th, ng	**7. Sound Dictation** sh, ch, th, ng
2. Focus Sound: sh With the consonant digraph phonemes play the 'grab game'. With the cards on the table the teacher says a sound and the pupils grab for the letter.	**8. Focus Sound: sh** • The teacher checks the letter formation for the correct start point, exit stroke and place on the line.
3. Blending (oral) Robot Speech: The teacher says the sounds, pupils say the word for dish, cash, gosh, crash, blush	**9. Phoneme Fingers:** The teacher says a word, pupils flick fingers for each phoneme in dish, cash, crash

4. Manipulating Sounds: With vowels a, e, i, o, u at the top of the board and consonants at the bottom, the teacher says a word. The pupils fold 'phoneme fingers and flick a finger for each phoneme in the word. One child comes up and makes the word. The teacher says the next word. The next child, after flicking 'phoneme fingers for the new word, changes 1 sound (or 2) makes the word and reads the new word.
- Today work on dish, dash, rash, crash, crush, blush or ship, shop, shot, shut, sham, shed

Reading	Spelling
5. Reading Words (cards) As per pack Step 2.1 E.g. dish, wish, dash, crash, smash	**10. Word Dictation** As per pack Step 2.1 E.g. dish, wish, dash, crash, smash
6. Reading Sentences (and controlled texts) As per pack Step 2.1 I can smash the dish. Tom shot the gun. I wish I had a ship. The shed is big	**11. Sentence Dictation** As per pack Step 2.1 I can smash the dish. Tom shot the gun. I wish I had a ship. The shed is big.

Comments (to inform next plan and IEP)

Consonant Digraph ch

Learning Objective: to blend and segment 3and 4 phoneme words with consonant digraph /ch/
Success Critieria: to read 3 & 4 phoneme words and sentences with the consonant digraph /ch/ and write dictated /ch/ words and sentences with 100 % accuracy.

Reading	Spelling
1. Review Sounds sh, ch, th, ng	**7. Sound Dictation** sh, ch, th, ng
2. Focus Sound: ch • With the consonant digraph phonemes play the 'grab game'. With the cards on the table the teacher says a sound and the pupils grab for the grapheme.	**8. Focus Sound: ch** • The teacher checks the letter formation for the correct start point, exit stroke and place on the line.
3. Blending (oral) Robot Speech: The teacher says the sounds r-i-ch, pupils listen and say the word for rich, such, chest, chimp	**9. Phoneme Fingers:** Teacher says word, pupils flick fingers for each sounds in r-i-ch, s-u-ch, ch-e-s-t, ch-i-m-p

• **4. Manipulating Sounds:** With vowels a, e, i, o, u at the top of the board and consonants at the bottom, the teacher says a word. The pupils fold 'phoneme fingers' and flick a finger up for each phoneme in the word. One child comes up and makes the word. The teacher says the next word. The next child, after flicking 'phoneme fingers for the new word, changes 1 sound (or 2), makes the word and reads the new word.
• Today work on chip, chap, chat, chop, chum, chug

Reading	Spelling
5. Reading Words (cards) See Sound Discovery Step 2.1 e.g. rich, such, chest, chimp, pinch	**10. Dictation Words (tap and write)** See Sound Discovery Step 2.1 e.g. rich, such, chest, chimp, pinch
6. Reading Sentences (and controlled texts) This is a big chest. The chimp is in the shed. I had a chop on a dish. I wish I had fish and chips.	**11. Dictation Sentences (pupils read words and sentences at the end)** This is a big chest. The chimp is in the shed. I had a chop on a dish. I wish I had fish and chips.

Comments (to inform next plan and IEP)

Consonant Digraph ng

Learning Objective: to blend and segment 3 and 4 phoneme words with consonant digraph /ng/
Success Critieria: to read 3 & 4 phoneme words and sentences with consonant digraph /ng/ and to write dictated /ng/ words sentences with 100 % accuracy.

Reading	Spelling
1. Review Sounds sh, ch, th, ng	**7. Sound Dictation** sh, ch, th, ng
2. Focus Sound: ng With consonant digraph phonemes play the 'grab game'. With the cards on the table the teacher says a sound and the pupils grab for the grapheme.	**8. Focus Sound: ng** The teacher checks the letter formation for the correct start point, exit stroke and place on the line.
3. Blending (oral) Robot Speech: The teacher says the sounds s-o-ng. Pupils listen and say the word for song, bring	**9. Phoneme Fingers:** Teacher says word, pupils flick fingers for each phoneme in, r-i-ng, s-o-ng, s-t-i-ng, b-r-i -ng

4. Manipulating Sounds: With vowels a, e, i, o, u at the top of the board and consonants at the bottom, the teacher says a word. The pupils fold 'phoneme fingers' and flick a finger up for each phoneme in the word, One child comes and makes the word. The teacher says the next word. The next child, after flicking 'phoneme fingers for the new word, changes 1 sound (or 2), makes the word and reads the new word.
  • Today work on gang, gong, long, song, sing, sting

Reading	Spelling
5. Reading Words (read from a pack) See Sound Discovery Step 2.1 Eg. hang, long, ring, cling, bring swing,	**10. Word Dictation** (tap and write) See Sound Discovery Step 2.1 Eg.hang, long, ring, cling, bring, swing
6. Reading Sentences (and controlled texts) I can bang on the drum. Can she sing a song? Jan got a ring in a box. This bit of string is long.	**11. Sentence Dictation** (pupils read words and sentences at the end) I can bang on the drum. Can she sing a song? Jan got a ring in a box. This bit of string is long.

Comments (to inform next plan and IEP)

Snappy Lesson Plan

Vowel Digraph ai

Learning Objective: to blend and segment 3 and 4 phoneme words with the vowel digraph/ai/

Success Critieria: to read 3 and4 phoneme words and sentences with the vowel digraph /ai/ and to write from dictation /ai/ words and sentences with 100 % accuracy.

Reading	Spelling
1. Review Sounds ch, th, sh, ng, ai, ee, ie, oa, ue	**7. Sound Dictation** ai, ee, ie
2. Focus Sound: ai Place all the above phoneme cards on the table, the teacher says a sound, pupils grab for the correct grapheme.	**8. Focus Sound**: ai The teacher checks the letter formation for the correct start point, exit stroke and place on the line.
3. Blending (oral) Robot Speech: The teacher says the sounds m-ai-n, the pupils listen and say the word for main, pain, train, stain, mail, rail	**9. Phoneme Fingers**: The teacher says a word and the pupils flick fingers for each sound in m-ai-n, p-ai-n, t-r-ai-l, s-t-ai-n
4. Manipulating Sounds: With vowel digraphs at the top of the board and consonants at the bottom, the teacher says a word. The pupils fold 'phoneme fingers' and flick a finger up for each phoneme in the word. One child comes up and makes the word. The teacher says the next word. The next child, after flicking 'phoneme fingers' for the new word, changes 1 sound (or 2), makes the word and reads the new word. • Today work on mail, main, rain, train, trail, snail	
5. Reading Words (read from a pack) See Sound Discovery Step 2.2 rain, stain, train, trail, brain, chain, paint	**10. Word Dictation** (tap and write) See Sound Discovery Step 2.2 rain, stain, train, trail, brain, chain, paint
6. Reading Sentences (and controlled texts) The train runs on rails. He had a pain in his left leg. I can wait for him at the ramp. I had to paint the box red.	**11. Sentence Dictation** (pupils read words and sentences at the end) The train runs on rails. He had a pain in his left leg. I can wait for him at the ramp. I had to paint the box red.
Comments (to inform next plan and IEP)	

Snappy Lesson Plan
Sound Discovery Step 2.2

Vowel Digraph ee

Learning Objective: to blend and segment3 and 4 phoneme words with the vowel digraph/ee/

Success Critieria: to read 3 and4 phoneme words and sentences with the vowel digraph /ee/ and to write from dictation /ee/ words and sentences with 100 % accuracy.

Reading	Spelling
1. Review Sounds ch, th, sh, ng, ai, ee, ie, oa, ue	**7. Sound Dictation** ai, ee, ie
2. Focus Sound: ee Place all the above phoneme cards on the table, the teacher says a sound, pupils grab for the correct grapheme.	**8. Focus Sound: ee .The teacher** checks the letter formation for the correct start point, exit stroke and place on the line.
3. Blending (oral) Robot Speech: The teacher says the sounds w-ee-p, the pupils listen and say the word for weep, sheet, see, steep, meet	**9. Phoneme Fingers:** The teacher says a word and the pupils flick fingers for each sound in w-ee-p, sh-ee-t, s-t-ee-p, m-ee-t
4. Manipulating Sounds: With vowel digraphs, at the top of the board and consonants at the bottom, the teacher says a word. The pupils fold 'phoneme fingers' and flick a finger up for each phoneme in the word. One child comes up and makes the word. The teacher says the next word. The next child, after flicking 'phoneme fingers' for the new word, changes 1 sound (or 2), makes the word and reads the new word. • Today work on seen, seed, deed, deep, steep, creep	
5. Reading Words (read from a pack) See Sound Discovery Step 2.2 weep, seen, seed, peel, creep, steep, fleet	**10. Word Dictation** (tap and write) See Sound Discovery Step 2.2 weep, seen, seed, peel, creep, steep, fleet
6. Reading Sentences (and controlled texts) I did not see the tramp in the shed. The sheep stands in the pen. Jim has a fleet of ships. This step is steep.	**11. Sentence Dictation** (pupils read words and sentences at the end) The train runs on rails. He had a pain in his left leg. I can wait for him at the ramp. I had to paint the box red.
Comments (to inform next plan and IEP)	

Snappy Lesson Plan

Sound Discovery Step 2.2

Vowel Digraph ie

Learning Objective: to blend and segment3 and 4 phoneme words with the vowel digraph/ie/

Success Critieria: to read 3 and4 phoneme words and sentences with the vowel digraph /ie/ and to write from dictation /ie/ words and sentences with 100 % accuracy.

Reading	Spelling
1. Review Sounds (show as a pack) ch, th, sh, ng, ai, ee, ie, oa, ue	**7. Sound Dictation** ai, ee, ie
2. Focus Sound: ie Place all the above phoneme cards on the table, the teacher says a sound, pupils grab for the correct grapheme.	**8. Focus Sound**: ie .The teacher checks the letter formation for the correct start point, exit stroke and place on the line.
3. Blending (oral) Robot Speech: The teacher says the sounds t-ie, the pupils listen and say the word for tie, pie, lie, ties, fried	**9. Phoneme Fingers**: The teacher says a word and the pupils flick fingers for each sound in t-ie, p-ie, l-ie, t-ie-s, f-r-ie-d

4. Manipulating Sounds: With vowel digraphs at the top of the board and consonants at the bottom, the teacher says a word. The pupils fold 'phoneme fingers' and flick a finger up for each phoneme in the word. One child comes up and makes the word. The teacher says the next word. The next child, after flicking 'phoneme fingers' for the new word, changes 1 sound (or 2), makes the word and reads the new word.
  - Today work on lie, pie, tie, ties, tried, fried

5. Reading Words (read from a pack) See Sound Discovery Step 2.2 tie, pie, lie, ties, fried	**10. Word Dictation** (tap and write) See Sound Discovery Step 2.2 tie, pie, lie, ties, fried
6. Reading Sentences (and controlled texts) I lie on my bed to go to sleep. Dad has a long red tie. Mum fried fish and chips in the pan. Tom tries to jump up the step.	**11. Sentence Dictation** (pupils read words and sentences at the end) I lie on my bed to go to sleep. Dad has a long red tie. Mum fried fish and chips in the pan. Tom tries to jump up the step.

Comments (to inform next plan and IEP)

Vowel Digraph oa

Learning Objective: to blend and segment 3 and 4 phoneme words with the vowel digraph /oa/

Success Critieria: to read 3 and 4 phoneme words and sentences with the vowel digraph /oa/ and to write from dictation /oa/ words and sentences with 100 % accuracy.

Reading	Spelling
1. Review Sounds (show as a pack) ch, th, sh, ng, ai, ee, ie, oa, ue	**7. Sound Dictation** ai, ee, ie, oa
2. Focus Sound: oa Place all the above phoneme cards on the table, the teacher says a sound, pupils grab for the correct grapheme.	**8. Focus Sound:** oa .The teacher checks the letter formation for the correct start point, exit stroke and place on the line.
3. Blending (oral) Robot Speech: The teacher says the sounds b-oa-t, the pupils listen and say the word for boat, foal, moan, coal, coat, foam	**9. Phoneme Fingers:** The teacher says a word and the pupils flick fingers for each sound in b-oa-t, f-oa-l, m-oa-n, c-oa-t, f-oa-m

4. Manipulating Sounds: With vowel digraphs at the top of the board and consonants at the bottom, the teacher says a word. The pupils fold 'phoneme fingers' and flick a finger up for each phoneme in the word. One child comes up and makes the word. The teacher says the next word. The next child, after flicking 'phoneme fingers' for the new word, changes 1 sound (or 2), makes the word and reads the new word.
  * Today work on foam, foal, coal, coat, moat, moan groan,

Reading	Spelling
5. Reading Words (read from a pack) See Sound Discovery Step 2.2 boat, foal, moan, coal, coat, foam	**10. Word Dictation** (tap and write) See Sound Discovery Step 2.2 boat, foal, moan, coal, coat, foam
6. Reading Sentences (and controlled texts) Get the coat from the peg, Tom. The boat sails on the foam. The foal stands in the hay. I cut my leg but I must not moan.	**11. Sentence Dictation** (pupils read words and sentences at the end) Get the coat from the peg, Tom. The boat sails on the foam. The foal stands in the hay. I cut my leg but I must not moan.

Comments (to inform next plan and IEP)

Snappy Lesson Plan   Sound Discovery Step 2.2
Vowel Digraph ue
Learning Objective: to blend and segment3 and 4 phoneme words with the vowel digraph/ue/
Success Critieria: to read 3 and4 phoneme words and sentences with the vowel digraph /ue/ and to write from dictation /ue/ words and sentences with 100 % accuracy.

Reading	Spelling
1. Review Sounds (show as a pack) ch, th, sh, ng, ai, ee, ie, oa, ue	**7. Sound Dictation** ai, ee, ie, oa, ue
2. Focus Sound: oa Place all the above phoneme cards on the table, the teacher says a sound, pupils grab for the correct grapheme.	**8. Focus Sound**: ue .The teacher checks the letter formation for the correct start point, exit stroke and place on the line.
3. Blending (oral) Robot Speech: The teacher says the sounds c-ue, the pupils listen and say the word for cue, due, rescue, statue, argue	**9. Phoneme Fingers**: The teacher says a word and the pupils flick fingers for each sound in cue, due, rescue, statue, argue

4. Manipulating Sounds: With vowel digraphs at the top of the board and consonants at the bottom, the teacher says a word. The pupils fold 'phoneme fingers' and flick a finger up for each phoneme in the word. One child comes up and makes the word. The teacher says the next word. The next child, after flicking 'phoneme fingers' for the new word, makes the word and reads the new word.

- Today work on cue, due, rescue, statue, argue, continue

Reading	Spelling
5. Reading Words (read from a pack) See Sound Discovery Step 2.2 cue, due, rescue, statue, argue	**10. Word Dictation** (tap and write) See Sound Discovery Step 2.2 cue, due, rescue, statue, argue
6. Reading Sentences (and controlled texts) The rent is due today. This is a snooker cue. Do not argue. I can see the statue.	**11. Sentence Dictation** (pupils read words and sentences at the end) The rent is due today. This is a snooker cue. Do not argue. I can see the statue.

Comments (to inform next plan and IEP)

Ridgehill Publishing© Tel (+44 or 0) 117 9622670
www.ridgehillpublishing.com

Snappy Lesson Plan
Vowel Digraph ar

Learning Objective: to blend and segment 3 and 4 phoneme words with the vowel digraph /ar/

Success Critieria: to read 3 and 4 phoneme words and sentences with the vowel digraph /ar/ and to write from dictation /ar/ words and sentences with 100 % accuracy.

Reading	Spelling
1. Review Sounds (show as a pack) ch, th, ng, ai, ee, ie, oa, ue, ar	**7. Sound Dictation** ai, ee, ie, oa, ue, ar
2. Focus Sound: ar Place all the above phoneme cards on the table, the teacher says a sound, pupils grab for the correct grapheme.	**8. Focus Sound**: ar .The teacher checks the letter formation for the correct start point, exit stroke and place on the line.
3. Blending (oral) Robot Speech: The teacher says the sounds c-ar, the pupils listen and say the word for cart, farm, garden, smart, star, park	**9. Phoneme Fingers**: The teacher says a word and the pupils flick fingers for each sound in cart, farm, garden, smart, star, park

4. Manipulating Sounds: With vowel digraphs at the top of the board and consonants at the bottom, the teacher says a word. The pupils fold 'phoneme fingers' and flick a finger up for each phoneme in the word. One child comes up and makes the word. The teacher says the next word. The next child, after flicking 'phoneme fingers' for the new word, changes 1 sound (or 2), makes the word and reads the new word.
  - Today work on car, cart, chart, charm, farm, farms

Reading	Spelling
5. Reading Words (read from a pack) See Sound Discovery Step 2.3 arm, star, farm, scarf, park, harsh	**10. Word Dictation** (tap and write) See Sound Discovery Step 2.3 arm, star, farm, scarf, park, harsh
6. Reading Sentences (and controlled texts) We went to the park. I can see the star in the sky. This chart is big and long. That is a smart bit of art.	**11. Sentence Dictation** (pupils read words and sentences at the end) We went to the park. I can see the star in the sky. This chart is big and long. That is a smart bit of art.

Comments (to inform next plan and IEP)

Snappy Lesson Plan

Vowel Digraph er

Learning Objective: to blend and segment3 and 4 phoneme words with the vowel digraph/er/
Success Critieria: to read 3 and4 phoneme words and sentences with the vowel digraph /er/ and to write from dictation /er/ words and sentences with 100 % accuracy.

Reading	Spelling
1. Review Sounds (show as a pack) ch, th, , ai, ee, ie, oa, ue,ar,or,er	**7. Sound Dictation** ai, ie, oa, ue, ar,er
2. Focus Sound: er Place all the above phoneme cards on the table, the teacher says a sound, pupils grab for the correct grapheme.	**8. Focus Sound**: er .The teacher checks the letter formation for the correct start point, exit stroke and place on the line.
3. Blending (oral) Robot Speech: The teacher says the sounds h-er-d, the pupils listen and say the word for term,herd,jerk,winter,clever,shelter	**9. Phoneme Fingers**: The teacher says a word and the pupils flick fingers for each sound in term,herd,jerk,winter,clever,shelter

4. Manipulating Sounds: With vowel digraphs at the top of the board and consonants at the bottom, the teacher says a word. The pupils fold 'phoneme fingers' and flick a finger up for each phoneme in the word. One child comes up and makes the word. The teacher says the next word. The next child, after flicking 'phoneme fingers' for the new word, makes the word and reads the new word.

- Today work on herd, jerk, clever, shelter, lobster

Reading	Spelling
5. Reading Words (read from a pack) See Sound Discovery Step 2.3 number, shelter, clever, hamper, jerk	**10. Word Dictation** (tap and write) See Sound Discovery Step 2.3 number, shelter, clever, hamper, jerk
6. Reading Sentences (and controlled texts) This is a bus shelter. His finger is cut. The cracker is in the hamper. Do not jerk the fishing rod.	**11. Sentence Dictation** (pupils read words and sentences at the end) This is a bus shelter. His finger is cut. The cracker is in the hamper. Do not jerk the fishing rod.

Comments (to inform next plan and IEP)

Ridgehill Publishing© Tel (+44 or 0) 117 9622670
www.ridgehillpublishing.com

Snappy Lesson Plan
Vowel Digraph or

Learning Objective: to blend and segment3 and 4 phoneme words with the vowel digraph/or/

Success Critieria: to read 3 and4 phoneme words and sentences with the vowel digraph /or/ and to write from dictation /or/ words and sentences with 100 % accuracy.

Reading	Spelling
1. Review Sounds (show as a pack) ch, th, , ai, ee, ie, oa, ue,ar,or	**7. Sound Dictation** ai, ie, oa, ue, ar
2. Focus Sound: or Place all the above phoneme cards on the table, the teacher says a sound, pupils grab for the correct grapheme.	**8. Focus Sound: or .**The teacher checks the letter formation for the correct start point, exit stroke and place on the line.
3. Blending (oral) Robot Speech: The teacher says the sounds p-or-t, the pupils listen and say the word for port, fork, horth, storm, torch, born	**9. Phoneme Fingers:** The teacher says a word and the pupils flick fingers for each sound in port, fork, horth, storm, torch, born

4. Manipulating Sounds: With vowel digraphs at the top of the board and consonants at the bottom, the teacher says a word. The pupils fold 'phoneme fingers' and flick a finger up for each phoneme in the word. One child comes up and makes the word. The teacher says the next word. The next child, after flicking 'phoneme fingers' for the new word, changes 1 sound (or 2), makes the word and reads the new word.

* Today work on corn, cork, pork, port, sport, sports

Reading	Spelling
5. Reading Words (read from a pack) See Sound Discovery Step 2.3 short,fork,torch,storm,sport,north	**10. Word Dictation** (tap and write) See Sound Discovery Step 2.3 short,fork,torch,storm,sport,north
6. Reading Sentences (and controlled texts) The storm is in the north. The stork stands on a leg. His shorts got torn. This torch is black.	**11. Sentence Dictation** (pupils read words and sentences at the end) The storm is in the north. The stork stands on a leg. His shorts got torn. This torch is black.

Comments (to inform next plan and IEP)

Ridgehill Publishing© Tel (+44 or 0) 117 9622670
www.ridgehillpublishing.com

Teaching Alternative Spellings   Sound Discovery Step 3A.2
Phoneme /ai / written as a-e, ai, ay

Learning Objective: to say 1 alternative spelling choice for phoneme /ai/, read it in words and sentences and write it in dictated words and sentences.

Success Criteria: to read 1 alternative spelling choice for phoneme /ai/ in words and sentences and to write that choice in dictated words and sentences with 100% accuracy.

a-e	ai	ay	ey
name	rain	pay	they
gate	stain	lay	grey
pale	grain	day	prey
tame	chain	tray	
rate	trail	play	
game	train	stay	
cake	paint	clay	

- The teacher draws the blank grid on the board and explains that today the class/group will be finding the main ways that the phoneme /ai/ can be written down.
- The pupils are asked to say 1 way e.g. **ai as in rain** and to say which column it goes into and the teacher writes the choice in the correct column.
- The pupils continue to generate examples with the teacher scribing the choice in the correct column until the columns are full.
- One child then comes to the board, reads the words in that column, underlines the pattern in a colour and comments on the position of the pattern in the word.
- The pupils come to the board in turn until all the alternative spelling patterns have been read, underlined and the position commented on.
- The children then draw the grid in their books and fill in the choices that will be referred to in subsequent lessons
- This lesson continues with the teacher choosing 1 alternative spelling pattern. **Today it is ai.** The grid is removed from the board and ai words and sentences are dictated as shown below.

rain	pain	rail
train	stain	trail
sail	paint	chain

  He had a pain in his left leg.
  I can wait for him next to the desk.
  I must not stand in the rain.
  The train runs on rails.
  Tom must paint the shed.
- After writing the dictation in their books, the pupils read it back.

Teaching Alternative Spellings   Sound Discovery Step 3A.2
Phoneme /ai / written as a-e, ai, ay

Learning Objective: to say 1 alternative spelling choice for phoneme /ai/, read it in words and sentences and write it in dictated words and sentences.

Success Criteria: to read 1 alternative spelling choice for phoneme /ai/ in words and sentences and to write that choice in dictated words and sentences with 100% accuracy.

a-e	ai	ay	ey
name	rain	pay	they
gate	stain	lay	grey
pale	grain	day	prey
tame	chain	tray	
rate	trail	play	
game	train	stay	
cake	paint	clay	

- The teacher draws the blank grid on the board and explains that today the class/group will be finding the main ways that the phoneme /ai/ can be written down.
- The pupils are asked to say 1 way e.g **ay as in pray** and to say which column it goes into and the teacher writes the choice in the correct column.
- The pupils continue to generate examples with the teacher scribing the choice in the correct column until the columns are full.
- One child then comes to the board, reads the words in that column, underlines the pattern in a colour and comments on the position of the pattern in the word.
- The pupils come to the board in turn until all the alternative spelling patterns have been read, underlined and the position commented on.
- The children then draw the grid in their books and fill in the choices that will be referred to in subsequent lessons
- This lesson continues with the teacher choosing 1 alternative spelling pattern. **Today it is ay.** The grid is removed from the board and ay words and sentences are dictated as shown below.

day	say	may
tray	play	stay
clay	pray	stray

Jim had a cup on the tray.

The hay is in the shed.

I can play with Tom.

Did he say yes?

He got the lump of clay from the box.

- After writing the dictation in their books, the pupils read it back.

Teaching Alternative Spellings   Sound Discovery Step 3A.2
Phoneme /ai / written as a-e, ai, ay

Learning Objective: to say 1 alternative spelling choice for phoneme /ai/, read it in words and sentences and write it in dictated words and sentences.

Success Criteria: to read 1 alternative spelling choice for phoneme /ai/ in words and sentences and to write that choice in dictated words and sentences with 100% accuracy.

a-e	ai	ay	ey
name	rain	pay	they
gate	stain	lay	grey
pale	grain	day	prey
tame	chain	tray	
rate	trail	play	
game	train	stay	
cake	paint	clay	

- The teacher draws the blank grid on the board and explains that today the class/group will be finding the main ways that the phoneme /ai/ can be written down.
- The pupils are asked to say 1 way e.g. **a-e as in game** and to say which column it goes into and the teacher writes the choice in the correct column.
- The pupils continue to generate examples with the teacher scribing the choice in the correct column until the columns are full.
- One child then comes to the board, reads the words in that column, underlines the pattern in a colour and comments on the position of the pattern in the word.
- The pupils come to the board in turn until all the alternative spelling patterns have been read, underlined and the position commented on.
- The children then draw the grid in their books and fill in the choices that will be referred to in subsequent lessons
- This lesson continues with the teacher choosing 1 alternative spelling pattern. **Today it is a-e**. The grid is removed from the board and a-e words and sentences are dictated as shown below.

cake	name	made
gate	lane	tape
came	late	take

His name is Jim.

I went to bed late.

Ben can make a cake.

The gate is at the end of the lane.

The tape is in the box.

- After writing the dictation in their books, the pupils read it back.

Teaching Alternative Spellings Sound Discovery Step 3A.4
Phoneme /ie/ written as ie, i-e, y, igh, i

Learning Objective: to say 1 alternative spelling choice for phoneme /ie/, read it in words and sentences and write it in dictated words and sentences.

Success Criteria: to read 1 alternative spelling choice for phoneme /ie/ in words and sentences and to write that choice in dictated words and sentences with 100% accuracy.

ie	y	igh	i-e	i
pie	my	high	line	wild
tie	by	light	five	mind
lie	try	night	kite	find
die	spy	fight	time	blind
untie	fly	fright	bike	mild
tries	sky	knight	pine	I
fried	shy	bright	ride	rind

- The teacher draws the blank grid on the board and explains that today the class/group will be finding the main ways that the phoneme /ie/ can be written down.
- The pupils are asked to say 1 way e.g. **ie as in pie** and to say which column it goes into and the teacher writes the choice in the correct column.
- The pupils continue to generate examples with the teacher scribing the choice in the correct column until the columns are full.
- One child then comes to the board, reads the words in that column, underlines the pattern in a colour and comments on the position of the pattern in the word.
- The pupils come to the board in turn until all the alternative spelling patterns have been read, underlined and the position commented on.
- The children then draw the grid in their books and fill in the choices that will be referred to in subsequent lessons
- This lesson continues with the teacher choosing 1 alternative spelling pattern. **Today it is ie.** The grid is removed from the board and ie words and sentences are dictated as shown below.

lie	untie	die
pie	fried	fries
tie	ties	tries

I lie in my bed.

Sam bit the pie with his teeth.

Tim can tie his long red tie.

Mum fried fish and chips in the pan.

Jan can untie this long bit of string

- After writing the dictation in their books, the pupils read it back.

Teaching Alternative Spellings   Sound Discovery Step 3A.4
Phoneme /ie/ written as ie, i-e, y, igh, i

Learning Objective: to say 1 alternative spelling choice for phoneme /ie/, read it in words and sentences and write it in dictated words and sentences.

Success Criteria: to read 1 alternative spelling choice for phoneme /ie/ in words and sentences and to write that choice in dictated words and sentences with 100% accuracy.

ie	y	igh	i-e	i
pie	my	high	line	wild
tie	by	light	five	mind
lie	try	night	kite	find
die	spy	fight	time	blind
untie	fly	fright	bike	mild
tries	sky	knight	pine	I
fried	shy	bright	ride	rind

- The teacher draws the blank grid on the board and explains that today the class/group will be finding the main ways that the phoneme /ie/ can be written down.
- The pupils are asked to say 1 way e.g. **y as in cry** and to say which column it goes into and the teacher writes the choice in the correct column.
- The pupils continue to generate examples with the teacher scribing the choice in the correct column until the columns are full.
- One pupil comes to the board, reads the words in that column, underlines the pattern in a colour and comments on the position of the pattern in the word.
- The pupils come to the board in turn until all the alternative spelling patterns have been read, underlined and the position commented on.
- The pupils draw the grid in their books and fill in the choices that will be referred to in subsequent lessons
- This lesson continues with the teacher choosing 1 alternative spelling pattern. **Today it is y.** That pattern is removed from the board and y words and sentences are dictated as shown below.

my	spy	cry
try	by	fry
sky	fly	sty

I can try to jump on the log.
The spy hid next to the tree.
He stands by the big desk
This is my red book and pen.
Jim cut his leg but he did not cry.

- After writing the dictation in their books, the pupils read it back.

Teaching Alternative Spellings Sound Discovery Step 3A.4
Phoneme /ie/ written as ie, i-e, y, igh, i

Learning Objective: to say 1 alternative spelling choice for phoneme /ie/, read it in words and sentences and write it in dictated words and sentences.

Success Criteria: to read 1 alternative spelling choice for phoneme /ie/ in words and sentences and to write that choice in dictated words and sentences with 100% accuracy.

ie	y	igh	i-e	i
pie	my	high	line	wild
tie	by	light	five	mind
lie	try	night	kite	find
die	spy	fight	time	blind
untie	fly	fright	bike	mild
tries	sky	knight	pine	I
fried	shy	bright	ride	rind

- The teacher draws the blank grid on the board and explains that today the class/group will be finding the main ways that the phoneme /ie/ can be written down.
- The pupils are asked to say 1 way e.g. **igh as in sight** and to say which column it goes into and the teacher writes the choice in the correct column.
- The pupils continue to generate examples with the teacher scribing the choice in the correct column until the columns are full.
- One pupil comes to the board, reads the words in that column, underlines the pattern in a colour and comments on the position of the pattern in the word.
- The pupils come to the board in turn until all the alternative spelling patterns have been read, underlined and the position is commented on.
- The pupils draw the grid in their books and fill in the choices that will be referred to in subsequent lessons
- This lesson continues with the teacher choosing 1 alternative spelling pattern. **Today it is igh.** The grid is removed from the board and **igh** words and sentences are dictated as shown below.

high	fight	fright
light	knight	bright
night	sight	slight

At night I lie in my bed and sleep.
The moon is big and bright tonight.
After his bad fright, he left the light on.
The knight sat on the bench until he had to fight.

- After writing the dictation in their books, the pupils read it back.

Teaching Alternative Spellings Sound Discovery Step 3A.4
Phoneme /ie/ written as ie, i-e, y, igh, i

Learning Objective: to say 1 alternative spelling choice for phoneme /ie/, read it in words and sentences and write it in dictated words and sentences.

Success Criteria: to read 1 alternative spelling choice for phoneme /ie/ in words and sentences and to write that choice in dictated words and sentences with 100% accuracy.

ie	y	igh	i-e	i
pie	my	high	line	wild
tie	by	light	five	mind
lie	try	night	kite	find
die	spy	fight	time	blind
untie	fly	fright	bike	mild
tries	sky	knight	pine	I
fried	shy	bright	ride	rind

- The teacher draws the blank grid on the board and explains that today the class/group will be finding the main ways that the phoneme /ie/ can be written down.
- The pupils are asked to say 1 way e.g. **i-e as in fine** and to say which column it goes into and the teacher writes the choice in the correct column.
- The pupils continue to generate examples with the teacher scribing the choice in the correct column until the columns are full.
- One pupil comes to the board, reads the words in that column, underlines the pattern in a colour and comments on the position of the pattern in the word.
- The pupils come to the board in turn until all the alternative spelling patterns have been read, underlined and the position commented on.
- The pupils draw the grid in their books and fill in the choices that will be referred to in subsequent lessons
- This lesson continues with the teacher choosing 1 alternative spelling pattern. **Today it is i-e.** The grid is removed from the board and i-e words and sentences are dictated as shown below.

line	spine	crime
five	time	spite
kite	bike	ride

  I can ride my bike up the steep hill.
  The pine trees bend in the strong wind.
  Tom will fly his kite on a long string.
  No mist, no rain, today it is fine.
- After writing the dictation in their books, the pupils read it back.

Teaching Alternative Spellings Sound Discovery Step 3A.4
Phoneme /ie/ written as ie, i-e, y, igh, i

Learning Objective: to say 1 alternative spelling choice for phoneme /ie/, read it in words and sentences and write it in dictated words and sentences.

Success Criteria: to read 1 alternative spelling choice for phoneme /ie/ in words and sentences and to write that choice in dictated words and sentences with 100% accuracy.

ie	y	igh	i-e	i
pie	my	high	line	wild
tie	by	light	five	mind
lie	try	night	kite	find
die	spy	fight	time	blind
untie	fly	fright	bike	mild
tries	sky	knight	pine	I
fried	shy	bright	ride	rind

- The teacher draws the blank grid on the board and explains that today the class/group will be finding the main ways that the phoneme /ie/ can be written down.
- The pupils are asked to say 1 way e.g. **i as in mind** and to say which column it goes into and the teacher writes the choice in the correct column.
- The pupils continue to generate examples with the teacher scribing the choice in the correct column until the columns are full.
- One pupil comes to the board, reads the words in that column, underlines the pattern in a colour and comments on the position of the pattern in the word.
- The pupils come to the board in turn until all the alternative spelling patterns have been read, underlined and the position commented on.
- The pupils draw the grid in their books and fill in the choices that will be referred to in subsequent lessons
- This lesson continues with the teacher choosing 1 alternative spelling pattern. **Today it is i.** The grid is removed from the board and i words and sentences are dictated as shown below.

mind	rind	hind
find	I	sign
mild	wild	miner

I can find my brush on the shelf.
No wind, no rain, it is mild today.
A fox is a wild animal.
This is the pig's hind leg.
I do not mind if that pen is lost.

- After writing the dictation in their books, the pupils read it back.

Teaching Alternative Spellings Sound Discovery Step 3A.5
Phoneme /oa/ written as o-e, oa, o, ow

Learning Objective: to say 1 alternative spelling choice for phoneme /oa/, read it in words and sentences and write it in dictated words and sentences.

Success Criteria: to read 1 alternative spelling choice for phoneme /oa/ in words and sentences and to write that choice in dictated words and sentences with 100% accuracy.

o-e	oa	o	ow
bone	boat	old	low
rope	road	no	bow
nose	coat	go	slow
spoke	goal	so	crow
stone	coast	most	snow
home	float	fold	flow
broke	toast	sold	grow

- The teacher draws the blank grid on the board and explains that today the class/group will be finding the main ways that the phoneme /oa/ can be written down.
- The pupils are asked to say 1 way e.g. **oa as in coat** and to say which column it goes into and the teacher writes the choice in the correct column.
- The pupils continue to generate examples with the teacher scribing the choice in the correct column until the columns are full.
- One child then comes to the board, reads the words in that column, underlines the pattern in a colour and comments on the position of the pattern in the word.
- The pupils come to the board in turn until all the alternative spelling patterns have been read, underlined and the position commented on.
- The children then draw the grid in their books and fill in the choices that will be referred to in subsequent lessons
- This lesson continues with the teacher choosing 1 alternative spelling pattern. **Today it is oa.** The grid is removed from the board and oa words and sentences are dictated as shown below.

boat	road	coat
goal	coast	float
toast	oak	soak

I cannot float yet.

She went to get a loaf from the shop.

Can you sit in the boat?

I had jam on my toast.

He got his coat from the peg.

- After writing the dictation in their books, the pupils read it back.

Teaching Alternative Spellings Sound Discovery Step 3A.5
Phoneme /oa/ written as o-e, oa, o, ow

Learning Objective: to say 1 alternative spelling choice for phoneme /oa/, read it in words and sentences and write it in dictated words and sentences.

Success Criteria: to read 1 alternative spelling choice for phoneme /oa/ in words and sentences and to write that choice in dictated words and sentences with 100% accuracy.

o-e	oa	o	ow
bone	boat	old	low
rope	road	no	bow
nose	coat	go	slow
spoke	goal	so	crow
stone	coast	most	snow
home	float	fold	flow

- The teacher draws the blank grid on the board and explains that today the class/group will be finding the main ways that the phoneme /oa/ can be written down.
- The pupils are asked to say 1 way e.g. **ow as in slow** and to say which column it goes into and the teacher writes the choice in the correct column.
- The pupils continue to generate examples with the teacher scribing the choice in the correct column until the columns are full.
- One child then comes to the board, reads the words in that column, underlines the pattern in a colour and comments on the position of the pattern in the word.
- The pupils come to the board in turn until all the alternative spelling patterns have been read, underlined and the position commented on.
- The children then draw the grid in their books and fill in the choices that will be referred to in subsequent lessons
- This lesson continues with the teacher choosing 1 alternative spelling pattern. **Today it is ow.** The grid is removed from the board and oa words and sentences are dictated as shown below.

low	bow	slow
crow	snow	grow
flow	show	throw
know	mow	blown

Seeds grow into plants.

The snow is deep next to the road.

I can mow the grass today.

This long train is slow.

The red box has a bow on it.

- After writing the dictation in their books, the pupils read it back.

Teaching Alternative Spellings Sound Discovery Step 3A.5
Phoneme /oa/ written as o-e, oa, o, ow

Learning Objective: to say 1 alternative spelling choice for phoneme /oa/, read it in words and sentences and write it in dictated words and sentences.

Success Criteria: to read 1 alternative spelling choice for phoneme /oa/ in words and sentences and to write that choice in dictated words and sentences with 100% accuracy.

o-e	oa	o	ow
bone	boat	old	low
rope	road	no	bow
nose	coat	go	slow
spoke	goal	so	crow
stone	coast	most	snow
home	float	fold	flow
broke	toast	sold	grow

- The teacher draws the blank grid on the board and explains that today the class/group will be finding the main ways that the phoneme /oa/ can be written down.
- The pupils are asked to say 1 way e.g. **o-e as in bone** and to say which column it goes into and the teacher writes the choice in the correct column.
- The pupils continue to generate examples with the teacher scribing the choice in the correct column until the columns are full.
- One child then comes to the board, reads the words in that column, underlines the pattern in a colour and comments on the position of the pattern in the word.
- The pupils come to the board in turn until all the alternative spelling patterns have been read, underlined and the position commented on.
- The children then draw the grid in their books and fill in the choices that will be referred to in subsequent lessons
- This lesson continues with the teacher choosing 1 alternative spelling pattern. **Today it is o-e.** The grid is removed from the board and oa words and sentences are dictated as shown below.

bone	rope	nose
spoke	stone	home
broke	mole	cone

The dog has a big bone.

He got on the bus to go home.

She held a long rope in her hand.

That bush has a red rose on it.

Tim hit Ron on the nose.

- After writing the dictation in their books, the pupils read it back.

Teaching Alternative Spellings Sound Discovery Step 3A.5
Phoneme /oa/ written as o-e, oa, o, ow

Learning Objective: to say 1 alternative spelling choice for phoneme /oa/, read it in words and sentences and write it in dictated words and sentences.

Success Criteria: to read 1 alternative spelling choice for phoneme /oa/ in words and sentences and to write that choice in dictated words and sentences with 100% accuracy.

o-e	oa	o	ow
bone	boat	old	low
rope	road	no	bow
nose	coat	go	slow
spoke	goal	so	crow
stone	coast	most	snow
home	float	fold	flow
broke	toast	sold	grow

- The teacher draws the blank grid on the board and explains that today the class/group will be finding the main ways that the phoneme /oa/ can be written down.
- The pupils are asked to say 1 way e.g. **o as in most** and to say which column it goes into and the teacher writes the choice in the correct column.
- The pupils continue to generate examples with the teacher scribing the choice in the correct column until the columns are full.
- One child then comes to the board, reads the words in that column, underlines the pattern in a colour and comments on the position of the pattern in the word.
- The pupils come to the board in turn until all the alternative spelling patterns have been read, underlined and the position commented on.
- The children then draw the grid in their books and fill in the choices that will be referred to in subsequent lessons
- This lesson continues with the teacher choosing 1 alternative spelling pattern. **Today it is o.** The grid is removed from the board and oa words and sentences are dictated as shown below.

old	no	go
sold	hold	so
host	most	fold

This cat is old and sick.

I sold my pens to Jim.

Go and get that book.

I can hold this long string.

Tom had the most sweets.

- After writing the dictation in their books, the pupils read it back.

Teaching Alternative Spellings Sound Discovery Step 3A.9
Phoneme /or/ written as or, au, aw, al

Learning Objective: to say 1 alternative spelling choice for phoneme /or/, read it in words and sentences and write it in dictated words and sentences.

Success Criteria: to read 1 alternative spelling choice for phoneme /or/ in words and sentences and to write that choice in dictated words and sentences with 100% accuracy.

or	au	aw	al
torch	sauce	saw	call
storm	cause	jaw	ball
north	haul	yawn	hall
shorts	launch	law	fall
shorter	because	dawn	chalk
stork	autumn	draw	small
horse	August	crawl	taller

- The teacher draws the blank grid on the board and explains that today the class/group will be finding the main ways that the phoneme /or/ can be written down.
- The pupils are asked to say 1 way e.g. **or as in port** and to say which column it goes into and the teacher writes the choice in the correct column.
- The pupils continue to generate examples with the teacher scribing the choice in the correct column until the columns are full.
- One pupil comes to the board, reads the words in that column, underlines the pattern in a colour and comments on the position of the pattern in the word.
- The pupils come to the board in turn until all the alternative spelling patterns have been read, underlined and the position commented on.
- The pupils draw the grid in their books and fill in the choices that will be referred to in subsequent lessons
- This lesson continues with the teacher choosing 1 alternative spelling pattern. **Today it is or.** The grid is removed from the board and i words and sentences are dictated as shown below.

port	north	torch	shorter	horse
storm	shorts	stork	northern	form

The storm is in the north.

The stork stands on the bank of the river.

Tom held the long, silver torch in his hand.

The ship sails into the port.

This boy is shorter than that boy.

I do not mind if that pen is lost.

- After writing the dictation in their books, the pupils read it back.

Selected Sound Discovery®
Snappy Lesson Plans

at Steps 1, 2 and 3A

This set of lesson plans has been written to support synthetic phonic teaching at Step 1, 2 and 3A of the Sound Discovery® programme. Teachers and teaching assistants can use these plans for whole class teaching and for group teaching.

Each plan has learning objectives, success criteria and clear instructions.

The plans should be used in conjunction with Sound Discovery® Placement Tests and the material in Sound Discovery® Words and Sentences Part .

ISBN: 1-84556-098-1